Dearest Cindy,

From one fashionista to another + my favorite partner in crime. One of my favorite books at the moment - hope you enjoy it :)

Happy Birthday!

♡ Karen
xo.

P.S plo don't leave — boo

FASHIONGAMEBOOK

© 2008 Assouline Publishing
601 West 26th Street, 18th Floor
New York, NY 10001 USA
Tel.: 212-989-6810   Fax: 212-647-0005
www.assouline.com

Translated from French by Barbara Mellor

ISBN: 978 2 75940 292 2

Color separation: Planète Couleurs (France)
Printed in China

FLORENCE MÜLLER

FASHIONGAMEBOOK
A WORLD HISTORY OF 20TH CENTURY FASHION

ASSOULINE

Coco Chanel used to say, "Fashion should really be followed, even if it is ugly. Moving away from fashion means the immediate and terrifying prospect of becoming laughable. No one is big enough to be above fashion." But it is more reasonable to say that one should understand the diversity of fashion and its many aspects that make its reign so difficult to avoid. It would be a pity not to embrace fashion, since it can be said, in its cycles and perpetual renewals, to symbolize life itself. This notion has been adopted in the contemporary era, which has finally seen the appropriation of many daily, artistic, and cultural objects.

FLORENCE MÜLLER

How to use this book

 Inspirations/Influences

 Perfumes

 Designers

 Labels

 Archetypal models

 Game

 Observation

 Question

 Answer

Contents

Designers' words
Who said what?